D1249620

A Gift of Angels

A Gift of Angels

20 Craft Projects for All Seasons

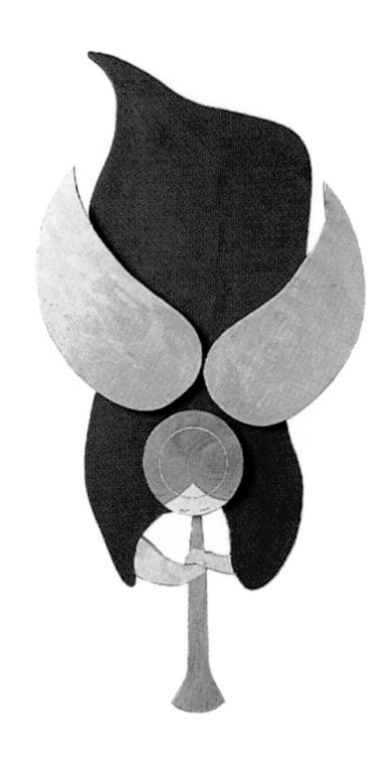

Brenda Browitt

Clarkson Potter/Publishers
New York

Published by Clarkson Potter/Publishers, 201 East 50th Street,
New York, New York 10022. Member of the Crown Publishing Group.

Random House, Inc. New York, Toronto, London, Sydney, Auckland

Manufactured in Hong Kong

Design by Susan DeStaebler

Library of Congress Cataloging-in-Publication Data
Browitt, Brenda
A gift of angels: 20 craft projects for all seasons /
Brenda Browitt. — 1st ed.
p. cm.
1. Handicraft. 2. Angels in art. I. Title.
TT157.P843 1995
745.594'1—dc20 94-46641
CIP

ISBN 0-517-70093-X

10 9 8 7 6 5 4 3 2 1

First Edition

This book is dedicated to God, the Creator of all things, including real angels.
May He grant you peace and joy as you craft yours.

Contents

Acknowledgments
8

Introduction
9

Door Wreath with
Apple & Spice Ornaments
10

Corn-Husk Angels
13

Trumpeting Angel
Door Hanging
16

Christmas Tree
with Angel Ornaments
19

Quilted Angel Pillow
22

Stained-Glass Ornament
and Window Hanging
25

Guardian Angel Pin
28

Paper Twist Angel
31

Christmas Stocking
35

Angelic Needlepoint Stocking
37

Angel in the Kitchen
40

Wedding Ring Pillow
43

Angelic Yard Flag
45

Angel Doll
48

Angel Tree Topper
50

Ribbon Bookmark
53

Halo of Flowers and Gold
54

Christmas Tree Skirt
56

Angel and Pine Tree Quilted Wall Hanging
59

Angel Blessing Box
62

Sources for Materials and Supplies
64

Acknowledgments

With love and thanks to the number-one angel in my life, my husband, Tom, for his help, especially with the power tools, and for his patience and support through the process of writing this book.

I am grateful to many friends for encouragement, inspiration, and evaluation. Especially Rich and Tina Telthorst; Lolly Murphy and Myrna Lawson for stained-glass lessons; Pam Davis for editing so that a noncrafter could understand the instructions; to Sue Tuminia, Marilyn Sones, Karen Schneider, Doris Engstrom, and Lisa Dimond for their enthusiasm and ideas. Many thanks to Julie Shay for helping hands, especially in styling photos. To Clare Dimond, hugs and kisses. You're my vision of the perfect three-year-old angel. My special thanks to Patricia Corrigan, who somehow knew, long before I was convinced, that I really could do this. And who then convinced her own agent, Jeanne Hanson, that I could, too. Thanks, Pat and Jeanne, for a heavenly trip.

Introduction

Angels are one of those everlasting symbols of love, like teddy bears and hearts, that are so comforting and familiar. I remember, as a child of seven or eight, making my first angel from cornstarch and salt "bread dough," measured and mixed by my mother at the kitchen table. Wings in a flying position, with garlic-pressed hair trailing behind her, she hung happily for many years among the plaster of Paris handprints and other treasures of childhood.

That first little angel has been replaced over the years with legions of others, twenty of which I share with you here. Some are simple projects you can make in an evening; others, like the Angelic Needlepoint Stocking, are more challenging. There are angels to grace your home during the holidays, as well as those you'll want to share in your life all through the year.

Nearly all the materials you will need are readily available in most craft and hobby stores, but I've also listed mail-order resources at the end of the book. You will also note that many of the patterns have of necessity been reduced. Most copying machines now enable you to punch in the percentage of enlargement or reduction you desire; simply enlarge the patterns as directed in each project to the proper size.

These crafts have been designed to encourage your own creativity. So have fun, and adapt or interchange the patterns and colors to suit yourself. Each angel deserves its own personality. I hope you will find one or two that inspire you to create a guardian angel of your own. And remember: when you share them with friends and loved ones, they will think you're an angel too.

Door Wreath with Apple & Spice Ornaments

*This lovely wreath will scent your home with spicy cinnamon and apple for many months. Make extra ornaments for your Christmas tree, too. Note: These ornaments are **not** edible.*

Materials for Spice Ornaments

½ cup cornstarch

2 1.9-ounce jars cinnamon

6 tablespoons ground cloves

1½ cups commercial applesauce

2 envelopes unflavored gelatin

angel cookie cutter (optional)

drinking straw

To Make the Spice Ornaments

1. In a mixing bowl, combine the cornstarch, cinnamon, and cloves. Set aside.
2. Combine the applesauce and gelatin in a saucepan and let sit for 4 minutes. Heat, stirring constantly, until just simmering. Remove from heat and pour over the cornstarch and spices. Stir well, and turn out onto a counter. Knead the dough several times, then wrap tightly in plastic wrap and let it rest for 10 minutes.
3. Divide and rewrap half the dough, then roll the other half out between two sheets of plastic wrap. Roll dough to about ¼-inch thickness.
4. Cut with a purchased angel cookie cutter, or enlarge the angel patterns on page 12 as indicated and make cardboard templates to trace around with a sharp knife. Use a drinking straw to make a decorative pattern on the skirt and a hole for hanging.
5. Allow ornaments to air-dry for two or three days on a wooden rack, turning each day.

To Make the Wreath

1. In a well-ventilated area, spray the wreath (but not the ornaments) with clear varnish. Let dry.
2. Weave the greenery, dried flowers, and narrow ribbon through the wreath in a pleasing pattern (Add fragile decorations such as the baby's breath after tying on the ornaments.) Secure with hot glue or wire.

Materials for Wreath

grapevine or twig wreath (purchased)

spray varnish

preserved greenery

baby's breath and other dried flowers

2 yards decorative ribbon, ½ inch wide

hot-glue gun and glue (optional)

thin florist's wire

2 yards 3-inch-wide wired ribbon

8 inches heavy wire for hanging

3. Make a large, simple bow from the wide wired ribbon and secure to the top of the wreath. Leave long tails and trim ends in an inverted V shape for a nice finish.
4. Tie seven or eight completely dried spice angel ornaments to the wreath, making sure they are secure.
5. Wire the back of the wreath with the heavy wire and hang inside to enjoy the apple and cinnamon scent, or outdoors in a protected area.

Angel is the only word in the language that can never be worn out.

—*Victor Hugo*

Large angel measures 5¾ inches tall
Enlarge both patterns 250%

Corn-Husk Angels

This Early American craft is both satisfying to make and easy to personalize when you use either natural or colored corn husks to vary the angel's robes. The angels shown here represent each of the four seasons. I like to use them as decoration on a large table or sideboard, but two or more in a beautiful basket lined with an antique linen towel or napkin also makes a spectacular centerpiece.

Instructions

1. Soak the corn husks in a bowl of warm water for a few minutes to make them easier to handle.
2. To make the head, cut two husks 1¾ inches wide and 6 or 7 inches long. Crisscross them tightly around the Styrofoam ball and secure with a piece of wire or raffia.
3. To make the arms, wrap a 6-inch piece of wire tightly with a husk 1½ inches wide and 7 inches long, again tying with wire or raffia, about ½ inch from each end, in the wrist position.
4. Use two overlapping pieces of husk, 4 inches square, for each sleeve. Gather the sleeve evenly around the arm, just above the wrist, and extending over the hand; secure the husks with wire.
5. Turn the two pieces of husk back on themselves, exposing the hand to form a puffed sleeve (see the illustration on page 34); secure at the shoulder position with wire or raffia.
6. Join the head and arms with wire, simply tying over and under the neck and arms in an X several times. Leave the husk below the neck to help form the torso.

Materials for One Angel

about 20 corn husks, natural or colored

Styrofoam ball, 1½ inches in diameter

32-gauge covered wire

raffia and string

hot-glue gun and glue

small amount of dried sphagnum moss, unspun wool, or cornsilk for hair

small basket, or bouquet of dried flowers for angel to hold

permanent marker pens

3-inch grapevine or Christmas wreath

6 inches stiff ribbon, ¼ inch wide

dried flowers, pinecone pieces, berries, leaves, and lace

7. To make dress top, use two pieces of husk, 2 by 6 inches. Cross the pieces over the shoulders and secure at the waist with wire.
8. To make the wings, use two pieces of husk, 3 by 7 inches. Fold each in half and secure together with raffia. Tie the wings to the angel's back at the waist with wire or raffia.
9. To make the skirt, use four or more large pieces of husk, approximately 4 by 6 inches. Gather them evenly around the waist with the skirt over the head and wings. Again, fold the husks back on themselves to make the full skirt. If you like a very full skirt, add more husks.
10. After you have arranged the skirt so that the pieces are overlapping and look pleasing, use a long piece of string to wrap and tie the skirt in place until it dries, overnight. If you want your angel to be in a sitting position, fold the skirt into that position and tie with string.
11. When dry, remove the string and trim the bottom of the skirt evenly so the angel will stand up.
12. Use a hot-glue gun to attach moss, unspun wool, or cornsilk for hair, or use a braid of raffia if you prefer.
13. Trim your angel with a small basket or bouquet of dried flowers. You may add a face with markers.
14. To make a halo for the top of the angel's head, start with the wreath as a base. Wrap the stiff ribbon around the wreath until it is completely covered, then hot-glue bits of dried flowers, pinecone pieces, berries, leaves, and lace to it.

A guardian angel o'er
his life presiding
Doubling his
pleasures, and his
cares dividing.

—*Samuel Rogers,*
"Human Life"

Trumpeting Angel Door Hanging

This simple wooden piece makes a wonderful housewarming or Christmas gift, or treat yourself to a charming, new front door ornament. Paint in muted Christmas colors, or select colors to coordinate with your home and leave the angel up all year to herald visitors.

Materials

6 square feet of 1-inch clear pine board

band saw or jigsaw

wood putty (optional)

sandpaper

selection of paints (exterior for an outdoor hanging)

fine-line permanent marker

oil-based antiquing stain (optional)

wood glue

3 1¼-inch wood screws

clear acrylic spray coating

heavy-duty picture hanger

Instructions

1. Enlarge the three pattern pieces to the desired size. (The angel pictured is 31 inches long or a 570% enlargement.) Trace the pattern pieces onto the pine board and cut out with a band saw or jigsaw. Use wood putty to fill any holes or gouges. Sand the pieces well on both sides and edges.
2. Using the photograph as a guide, paint the pieces. Lighter colors may require two coats of paint. Allow to dry overnight. Use the fine-line marker to draw on the halo. If you want a more primitive look, antique the pieces with antiquing stain. Rubbing the painted edges back to raw wood with sandpaper before applying the stain will heighten the effect.
3. Apply wood glue to the head and wings and position on the body. When dry, use wood screws to further secure the wings and head from the back. (This is especially important if you plan to hang the angel on the outside of your door.)
4. Apply two or three coats of acrylic spray to protect the angel.
5. Screw a heavy-duty picture hanger into the back, about 6 inches from the top.

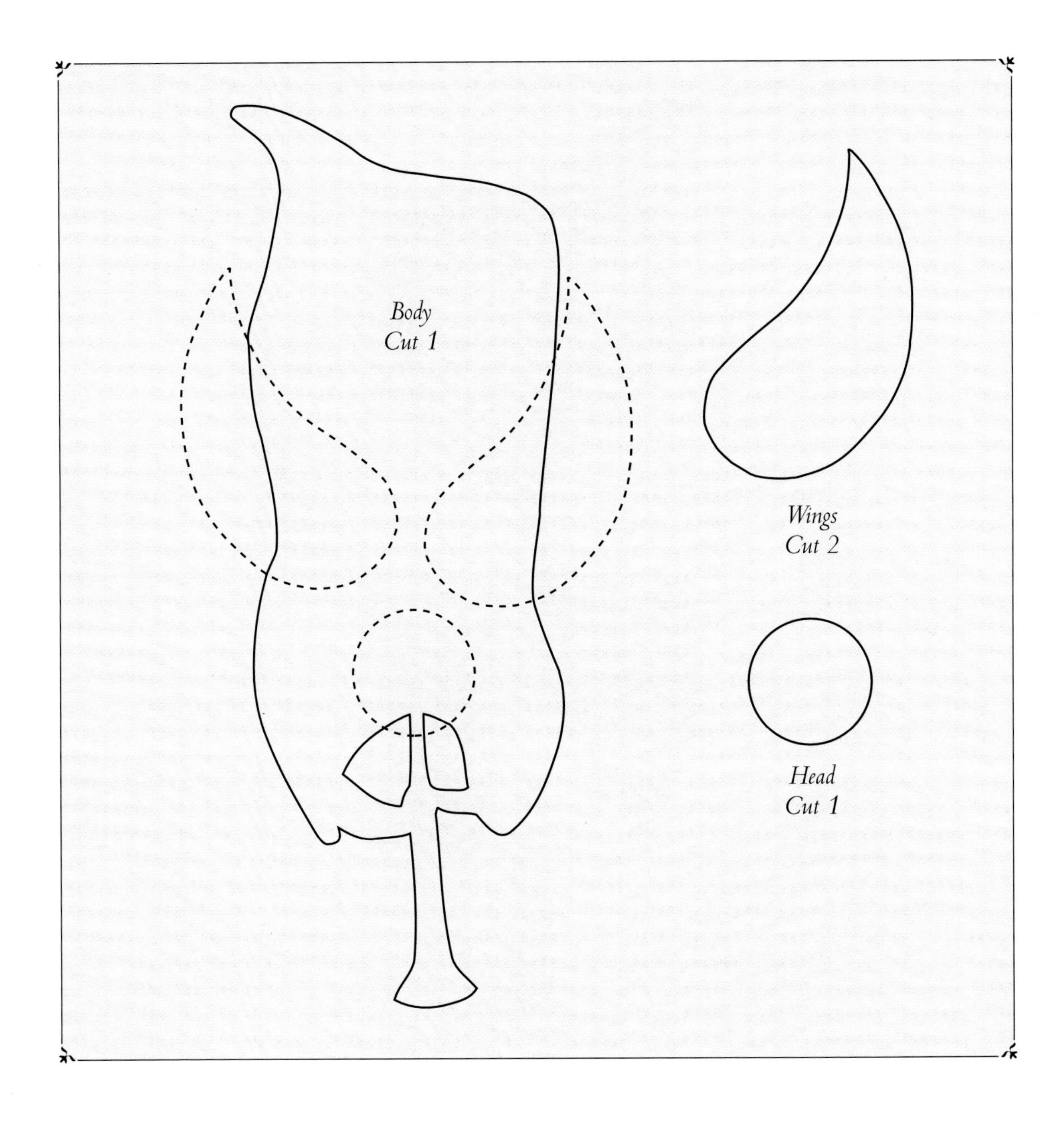
Body
Cut 1
Wings
Cut 2
Head
Cut 1

Christmas Tree with Angel Ornaments

This 3-foot tree is very similar to old Victorian feather trees. Cut your own ornaments or purchase precut wooden blanks at a craft store and decorate to taste. Use the angel patterns to make cardboard templates for cutting out holiday cookies, or as stencils and stamps for making gift wrap.

To Make the Tree

1. Use the ⅜-inch bit to drill four parallel holes into the large dowel rod at 3, 11, 19, and 26 inches from the top. With a saw, cut the ⅜-inch dowel rods to 13-, 18-, 23-, and 28-inch lengths. Sand the ends flat. Insert the ⅜-inch dowel rods through the holes in the large dowel and center them. They should fit snugly.
2. If desired, cut the pine board for the base into a circle or hexagon and sand all sides well. Drill a ¾-inch hole into the center of the base, insert the large dowel rod, and glue. Allow to dry overnight.
3. In a well-ventilated place, spray the entire tree, including the base, with the green enamel paint. When dry, sand and apply antiquing glaze if you like. Allow to dry again, then spray with clear acrylic coating. Dry thoroughly.

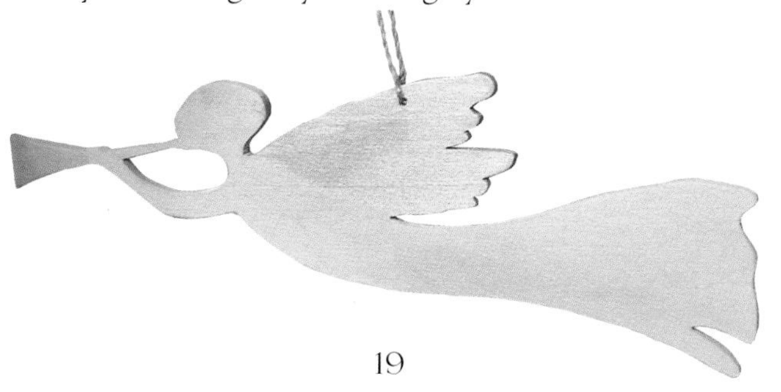

Materials for Tree

- hand or power drill with ⅜- and ¾-inch drill bits
- 1 ¾-inch dowel rod, 36 inches long
- small handsaw or jigsaw
- 3 ⅜-inch dowel rods
- fine-grit sandpaper
- 1-inch clear pine board, at least 10 inches square, for base
- wood glue
- forest green enamel spray paint
- antiquing glaze (optional)
- clear acrylic spray coating
- 4 yards artificial pine roping, single width
- hot-glue gun and glue
- shears or heavy-duty scissors

Materials for Ornaments

$\frac{1}{4}$-inch basswood, pine, or ash, or heavy chipboard cardboard, about 3 square feet

pencil

small handsaw or jigsaw

drill with $\frac{1}{8}$-inch bit

fine-grit sandpaper

water-based paints in a selection of colors, including metallic gold and silver

water-based antiquing glaze (optional)

clear acrylic spray coating

tiny purchased accessories, such as horns, dried flowers, snowflakes, or greenery

1 yard twine

4. Starting at the base of the tree, wrap the pine roping around the tree-trunk, using hot glue to secure every few inches. Cut with shears when you get to the top and proceed to wrap each branch, again securing with hot glue.

To Make the Angel Ornaments

1. Enlarge the patterns as indicated. Cut out and trace onto the wood or cardboard with a pencil.
2. With the saw, cut out the ornament shapes. Drill a $\frac{1}{8}$-inch hole in the top of each for hanging. Sand all sides well.
3. Be sure angels are free of wood dust and grit, then paint both sides of each. Light colors may take two coats to cover. If you like a more rustic look, sand the edges of your painted angels and antique them with a water-based glaze, wiping off as much or as little of the glaze as you like.
4. When the angels are dry, spray both sides with clear acrylic coating and allow to dry again. Decorate with tiny accessories if you like.
5. Use twine to tie the ornaments onto the tree.

Enlarge patterns 250%

Quilted Angel Pillow

This cream-on-cream muslin quilted pillow makes a lovely bridal shower gift that will blend with any color or style the newlyweds might choose. These also make nice accent pillows, especially with a scattering of other pieced or quilted pillows in different shapes. This pillow is 16 inches square, but the pattern will adapt to any size you prefer.

Materials

water-erasable blue marker

3 18 by 18-inch squares preshrunk cotton muslin, ironed

18 by 18-inch square low-loft quilt batting or fusible batting

14-inch embroidery or quilting hoop

quilting sharps or needle

natural-colored heavy-duty quilting thread

2 different cotton laces, 2 yards each for edging

16-inch pillow form

Instructions

1. Use a copier to enlarge the pattern on page 24 by 175%, or to fit your pillow. Using a water-erasable blue marker, copy the pattern onto one of the muslin squares, right side up. A light table or slide light box is helpful; alternatively, tape the pattern and fabric to a window to see the design through the muslin.
2. Assemble the pillow top in three layers, with batting between the patterned top and a backing of another plain muslin square; baste by hand to hold in place. If you use fusible batting, simply iron the pieces together.
3. Stretch the pillow top in the embroidery hoop. Thread quilting sharps or needle with quilting thread. Using a small running stitch, quilt over the design, beginning at the center of the design and working toward the outer edges. Use small, even stitches—they are the focal point of this project.
4. When you've finished quilting, wash out the pattern marks. Allow the pillow top to dry, then gently iron on the wrong side.
5. Baste the two lace edgings onto the pillow top, aligning the edges so the ruffles face toward the center. Top with the third

muslin square, right sides together, and machine-stitch around all four sides, leaving 8 inches open on one side to allow easy turning and fitting of the pillow form. Be careful to trap only the edges of the lace in the seam; double-seam for strength.

6. Trim the seams to ¼ inch. Turn the pillow cover right side out.
7. Insert the pillow form, and blind-stitch the opening closed.

So in a voice, so in
a shapeless flame
Angels affect us oft,
and worshipped be.

—*John Donne*

Stained-Glass Ornament and Window Hanging

Stained-glass making is a relatively easy craft to learn, and the supplies are inexpensive and widely available. The simple angel ornament on page 27 makes a great hostess gift. Make several in different colors to hang on a tree or in a window. The larger, more intricate hanging below is beautiful for a foyer.

Materials

cardboard for pattern

masking tape

workboard

glass-cutter scissors

white and black glass markers

stained glass in assorted colors

oil cutter

pliers

glass grinder

copper foil

metal pushpins

flux and brush

soldering iron and solder

patina and brush

purchased wire hangers

brass chain, picture wire, or heavy-duty fishing line

Instructions

1. Enlarge the pattern on page 27 as indicated, or to the desired size, then trace onto a piece of cardboard. Tape the original paper copy to your workboard surface. Cut the cardboard pattern pieces apart with glass-cutter scissors, which cut the pieces slightly smaller, allowing for the copper foil width.

Outside the open window the morning air is all awash with angels.

—*Richard Wilber, from "Love Call Us to the Things of This World"*

2. Using the markers, carefully trace the cardboard pattern pieces onto your glass. You will need these lines for both cutting and grinding. Mark each piece with the corresponding pattern number to assemble correctly.
3. Cut the glass pieces carefully using the oil cutter, scoring the glass in as straight a line as possible, and breaking down and away from the score line with pliers. Cut from one edge of glass all the way to the other to avoid jagged breaks.
4. After all pieces are cut, use the grinder to smooth all edges exactly to the pattern lines. Check your fit by placing pieces on the pattern attached to your workboard. When you are sure they fit together, you're ready to begin assembly. Wipe the glass pieces off with a paper towel.
5. Unroll and peel the backing from the copper foil a little at a time, as you encase the edges of each glass piece evenly. It is important to have the same amount of foil on both sides of the glass.
6. Again check the fit of the foiled pieces by placing on top of the traced pattern. Use metal pushpins to hold the pieces together on the workboard.
7. Lightly flux each edge of copper foil that you can see, using a brush that is reserved for flux. Preheat your soldering iron.
8. Hold the soldering iron close to the solder to allow the melted solder to flow over the copper foil, joining the pieces of glass together. If the solder gets a few lumps, simply run the iron over it again to smooth out the finish. You want a nice raised

bead of solder over all the copper-foil seams. Allow the joints to cool before removing the pins.

9. When cool, turn the angel over and repeat the flux and soldering steps on the reverse side. Attach a fluxed wire hanger to the top of the halo with a drop of solder. Cool again and carefully wash the piece with soap and water.
10. With a separate brush, apply patina to the soldered joints. When it is dark enough to suit you, dry it off and attach picture hooks and brass chain to the hanging and picture wire or fishing line to the ornament.

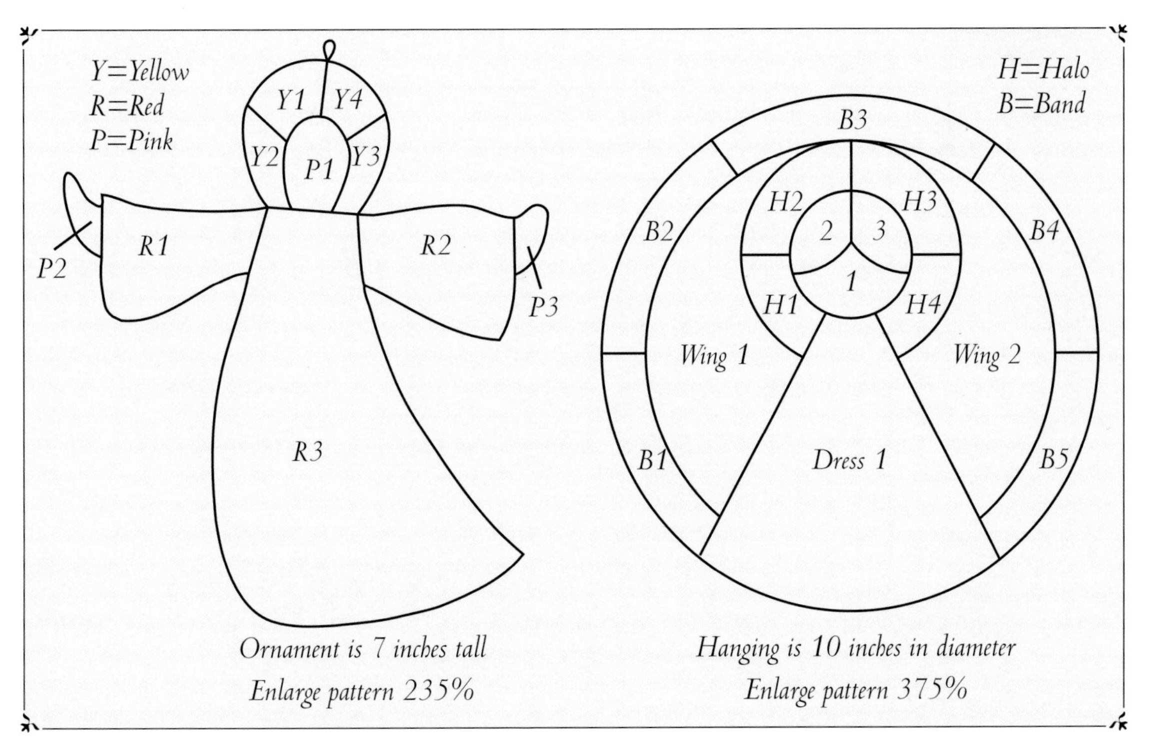

Ornament is 7 inches tall
Enlarge pattern 235%

Hanging is 10 inches in diameter
Enlarge pattern 375%

MATERIALS

modeling compound (air-dry type)

water-based paints

needlepoint yarn for hair

hot-glue gun and glue

plain muslin scraps for angel body

embroidery floss

darning needle

polyester fiberfill

miniprint cotton scraps for dress

tiny lace, beads, or glitter for decoration

gold braid or elastic for halo

decorative dried flowers, charms, or a basket

4-inch piece of wired ribbon for wings

pinback (purchased)

GUARDIAN ANGEL PIN

Make several of these charming little angels from scraps in your sewing basket. You'll love wearing one on your own shoulder, and they make unique gifts for teachers and special friends.

INSTRUCTIONS

1. Use modeling compound to form a small head and face about 3/8 inch in diameter. A toothpick works well to help model the face, but keep it simple in this small size. Allow to air-dry overnight, and then paint on features with water-based paints.
2. Using three strands of needlepoint yarn, work a simple braid about 2¼ inches long, tying off both ends. Glue the braid around the head in a spiral; leave the braided ends hanging like pigtails, or wind them into a topknot and secure with glue.
3. Trace the pattern for the legs (which includes the body) and the arms onto a piece of plain muslin. Cut four leg/body pieces and four arms. Stitch by hand or by machine, leaving an opening to turn right side out. It is helpful to catch a piece of embroidery floss or string into the seams at the toe and fingers. You can then use the floss to help pull when you turn these pieces to the right side. Trim the seams to 1/8 inch, clipping the curves, and turn to right side.
4. With a toothpick or darning needle, firmly stuff the arms and legs with fiberfill. Hand-sew the top of the legs together at the front and back seams to form the body. Hot-glue the arm openings to the body. Glue the head to the body.

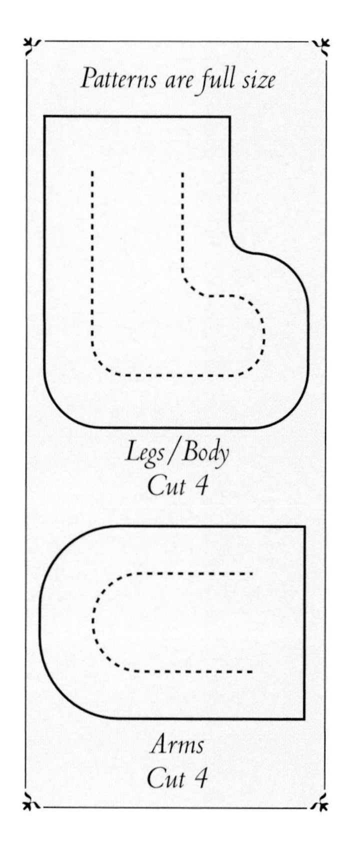

5. To make the dress, use two pieces of miniprint fabric, 1½ by 1¼ inches, and press a ¼-inch hem along one long edge of each piece of fabric. With right sides together, stitch both short sides from the unhemmed edge to within a ¼ inch of the hemed edge; this opening is for the angel's arms. If you wish, decorate the dress with lace, beads, glitter, or embroidery. Run a gathering stitch around the hemmed edge of the dress and, leaving the needle attached, position the dress over the arms. Gather the neckline and secure to the body with a couple of stitches. Add a lace apron if desired.
6. Use a 1-inch piece of gold braid or elastic thread to form a halo and secure with a stitch to the hair. Glue dried flowers, charms, or a tiny basket to either hand.
7. Join the wired ribbon at the ends and gather in the center to form two wings. Stitch the wings to the angel's back.
8. Sew the pinback to the center of the wings.

Paper Twist Angel

This angel is fun and inexpensive to make. Adjust the colors and trim to suit your fancy or the occasion. It's shown here as a romantic Valentine centerpiece with heart-shaped buttons, ribbons, and red roses.

Instructions

1. Fill the bottle about halfway with sand or kitty litter. Insert the dowel in the sand until it hits the bottom of the bottle (it should protrude at least 1½ inches). Mark the point on the dowel where it touches the rim. Withdraw the dowel partially and wrap masking tape below the mark. Continue wrapping the tape over on itself, keeping it smooth, to form a stopper to hold the dowel in place. It should fit securely. Hot-glue the stopper into the bottle neck. (See illustration on page 34.)
2. Untwist a section of the wide paper ribbon and cut a piece about 14 inches square to cover the bottle. Spread a thin layer of white glue on the bottle and wrap the smoothed piece of paper ribbon around it to cover. Tuck the bottom ends up as if you were wrapping a package. Trim and glue securely at the bottle neck, and let dry overnight.
3. Untwist another piece of wide paper ribbon, about 5 by 10 inches. Cover the Styrofoam ball with a thin coat of white glue and work the paper smoothly around it. Tie or rubber-band the paper ends together and let dry. Trim flat and push the tied end onto the dowel until it meets the bottle neck. Remove, then apply glue to the dowel and hole and resecure. Let dry.

Materials

1-liter plastic bottle

2 cups sand or kitty litter to weight bottle

1 ⅜-inch dowel rod

masking tape

hot-glue gun and glue

twisted paper ribbon in narrow and wide widths

white craft glue

3-inch Styrofoam ball

craft wire

craft moss

8 to 10 inches gold or silver garland or ribbon for halo

small dried flowers

decorative holly, silk rosettes, heart, or other trinkets

lace and ribbons (optional)

4. Dress the angel with a paper underskirt by forming a 12 by 2-inch piece of the wide paper into a tube shape, gathering and securing to the bottle neck with hot glue. Make the frilled collar with two 3 by 9-inch paper pieces, glued at the neck and standing up to make a ruffled collar in front and back. For the apron, glue a piece of untwisted large paper, 8 by 16 inches to the underskirt at the neck. (See photograph for positioning of clothing.)
5. Make arms by cutting a piece of the still-twisted narrow paper 16 inches long. Wrap it with wire for strength. For the sleeves, form a 6 by 16-inch piece of untwisted paper into a narrow tube and glue. Cut it in half. Insert 1 inch of each arm into a tube and tie or wire it at the wrist. Fold the tube back on itself to form puffed sleeve. (See illustration on page 34.) Hot-glue the arms to the body back.
6. Use a piece of untwisted paper, 40 inches long, to tie a cummerbund over the apron. Knot it in back and make a large bow to form wings. Leave long ties and trim in V shape to finish the ends.
7. Use craft moss for hair, hot-gluing in place. Form a halo from garland or ribbon. Secure to the head in several places with more glue and decorate with dried flowers. Add holly or silk rosettes to the hands, or use a purchased tiny heart, candle, or other trinkets to give your angel her own personality. You can adapt these instructions and make angels in different sizes or colors and with contrasting colors for apron or sleeves. Be creative and add lace or ribbons as you like for seasonal or special occasion looks.
8. Fluff out the skirt, apron, and wings. Position the arms, and your centerpiece is ready to grace a table or mantelpiece.

What might appear
as an angel may be
your love in disguise.

—*Anonymous*

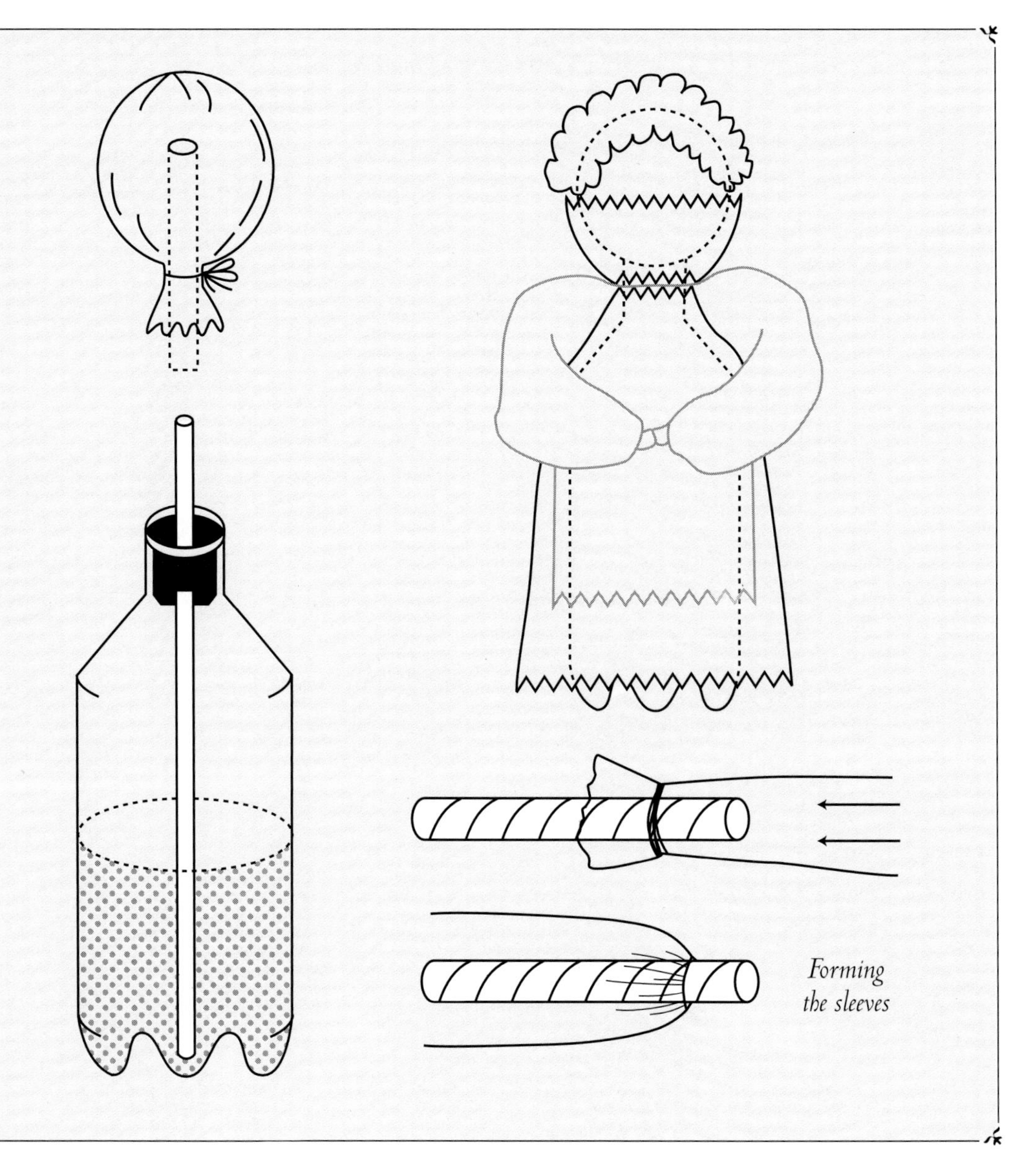
Forming
the sleeves

Christmas Stocking

This little angel waits patiently in the clouds for Christmas Eve when Santa comes to fill her stocking. It's fun when hung on the child's bedpost, in the European tradition. Add your angel's name with a marker or embroidery.

Instructions

1. Enlarge the pattern on page 36 by 330%.
2. With the bonding material, heat-bond the wrong sides of fabric and felt pieces for the dress, hair, cheeks, face, hands, and wings. Trace the patterns onto the bonded side.

Materials

¼ yard iron-on fabric bonding

10-inch piece of flannel, wool, or printed felt for dress

felt squares in pink, tan, blue, and rose

tracing paper

sewing scissors

½ yard white felt for stocking

embroidery needle and floss to match felt colors

3 small decorative bells

3 pieces velvet ribbon to match dress fabric

plastic curtain ring for hanging

plastic snowflakes

Hush! my dear,
lie still and slumber,
Holy angels guard
thy bed!
Heavenly blessing
without number
Gently falling on
thy head.

—*Isaac Watts*
Divine Songs

3. Cut out each pattern piece and remove the paper backing.
4. Freehand, draw a stocking pattern as wide as the angel's sleeves and 16 inches long. Cut a front and back from the white felt. Remove the top 3 inches of the back piece.
5. Embroider outlines of clouds onto the front of the stocking in light blue, using a chain stitch and three strands of floss.
6. Assemble the angel face, cheeks, and hair to the wings by following the ironing instructions on the bonding material. Bond entire head, dress, and hands to stocking front.
7. Embroider edges of wings, hair, hands, and dress to the stocking front, using a simple blanket stitch and matching floss colors.
8. Machine-stitch the right side of the front to the back of the stocking from just below the arms, leaving ¼-inch seams.
9. Sew bells to the ribbons and the ribbons to the angel's hands.
10. Sew a plastic curtain ring to the center back to hang the stocking.
11. Hot-glue the snowflakes randomly onto the clouds.

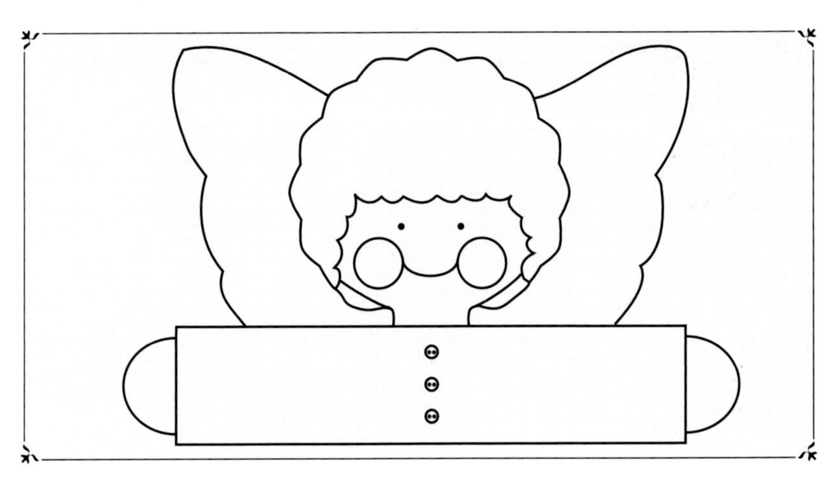

Angelic Needlepoint Stocking

Here's a beautiful Christmas angel stocking, a labor of love, and heirloom for that very special angel in your life. The stocking in the photo was worked in a combination of perle cotton and needlepoint wool, and includes some highlighting with metallic thread, but you may use regular embroidery floss, all wool, or a combination. Personalize with a name.

Instructions

1. Enlarge the pattern on page 38 as indicated.
2. Use masking tape to bind the edges of the canvas to prevent it from fraying; allow for a ½-inch seam allowance on all sides of the stocking. Carefully transfer the complete pattern onto the canvas using a felt-tip pen to outline the pattern, and waterproof-colored markers to indicate the sections of color. Take a little time at this stage because it will help you avoid constantly referring to the pattern as you are stitching.
3. Select your colors of embroidery floss, perle cotton, or needlepoint wool and using a tapestry needle work the full angel design in a single continental stitch. Work the angel wings in a double continental or bargello stitch, if you like, for a different texture. The background may also be worked in this manner.
4. If your stocking becomes slightly misshapen from the stitching, steam press the back of the canvas, using a damp towel to protect the stitching.
5. Using the needlepoint design as your pattern plus 2½ inches extra

Materials

masking tape

12 by 22-inch piece of 14-count needlepoint canvas

felt-tip pen

waterproof-colored markers

embroidery floss, perle cotton, or needlepoint wool, 1 or 2 skeins of each color

tapestry needles

⅓ yard cotton velveteen

⅓ yard acetate or nylon lining fabric, in a coordinating color

scissors

18 inches of heavy, 3-inch flat lace

1 yard velvet ribbon

DMC Colors

Hair: 739, 738, 436

Skin: 353, 754

Cheeks: 761

Ribbons: 3045, 3046

Gold Cloisonné, 100% polyester, nontarnishing thread

Robe: 498, 815, 902

Underdress: 500, 501

Wings: 822, 712

Background: Hunter green wool, 660

Flower garland/halo: 987, 899, 712

at the top, cut a backing for the stocking from the velveteen and two lining pieces from the lining fabric. Stitch the lining together, pressing seams open; do not turn.

6. Cut a cuff 6 by 16 inches, out of the velveteen. Hand-stitch the lace along the 16-inch side, about $\frac{3}{4}$ of an inch from the raw edge. With right sides together, machine-stitch the 6 inch sides together with a $\frac{1}{2}$-inch seam. Press the seam open. Fold in half lengthwise with wrong sides together to form a finished cuff.
7. Align the back to the needlepointed front, right sides together, and machine-stitch around the stocking, leaving the top open. Trim seams, clip curves, and press open, again using a towel to protect the stitching. Turn the stocking right side out.
8. Fit the cuff inside the lining, right sides together, with raw edges aligned. Stitch and press the seam allowance toward the lining. Insert the lining into the stocking fitting smoothly. You may want to blindstitch the toe and heel inside the seam, to secure the lining to the stocking. Fold the cuff down over the stocking and blindstitch in place.
9. Fold the velvet ribbon in half and tack to the side seam, allowing a 4-inch loop to extend above the cuff as a hanger.

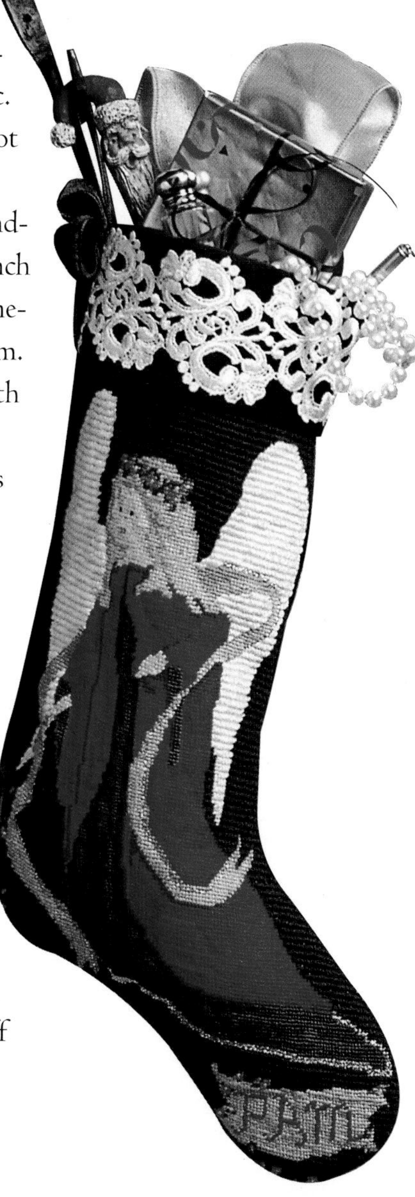

Angel in the Kitchen

Hang this raffia angel in your kitchen for heavenly inspiration. She's great company for the cook, but don't ask her to do the dishes.

Materials

large package of long raffia, natural color

craft glue or spray fixative

3-inch Styrofoam ball

wire or twist tie

hot-glue gun and glue

small dried flowers

small cinnamon stick pieces, nutmegs, or other small whole spices

¼ yard printed cotton fabric for dress

½ yard white lace, about ½ inch wide

3 by 3-inch square of cotton fabric for basket lining

small purchased basket for angel to hold

6 or 8 mixed nuts

Instructions

1. Divide the package of raffia into thirds. Apply craft glue or spray fixative to the Styrofoam ball, then cover with one-third of the raffia to form the head and body. Stretch the raffia over the ball and tie under the chin with a piece of wire or twist tie. Keep it as smooth as possible for an even face surface.
2. Divide the second one-third of the raffia in half for the arms. Make each arm by folding the raffia in half. With a single piece of raffia, tie about 1½ inches above the fold, at the wrist position. Tie again, 4 inches from the fold, to indicate the elbow. Tie again at the shoulder, 10 inches above the fold. About 10 or 12 inches of raffia will be left hanging. Braid these remaining inches of raffia to form the halo base. (You can adjust if necessary by cutting the raffia or braiding in an extra length.)
3. Tie the arms to the body and neck at the shoulder position, leaving the braided ends free. Twist the two braids together to form the halo and hot-glue to secure. The halo should be about 1 inch above the angel's head.
4. Hot-glue dried flowers and cinnamon pieces or other small spices to the braid to decorate the halo.
5. Enlarge the dress pattern on page 42 as indicated. Trace onto the dress fabric, cut out, and sew, right sides together, using ½-inch

Every man hath a good and a bad angel attending on him in particular, all his life long.

—*Robert Burton "Anatomy of Melancholy"*

seams. Turn and add a row of lace to finish the arms, hem, and neck edges. Leave the back open to allow for wings. Put dress on angel.

6. Using the final one-third of raffia, tie a large simple bow and secure tightly in the middle. Trim off the loose ends and tie securely to the angel body, forming the wings. If necessary, additional reinforcement with hot glue will keep the wings and arms in the correct position. Attach a doubled length of raffia, 6 inches long, for hanging the angel.
7. Fray the ends of the 3 by 3-inch fabric and use it to line the purchased basket. Fill the basket with mixed nuts and hot-glue them in place. Attach the basket to the angel's hand. Customize the angel with other ornaments, such as a small wooden apple or rolling pin, if you wish.

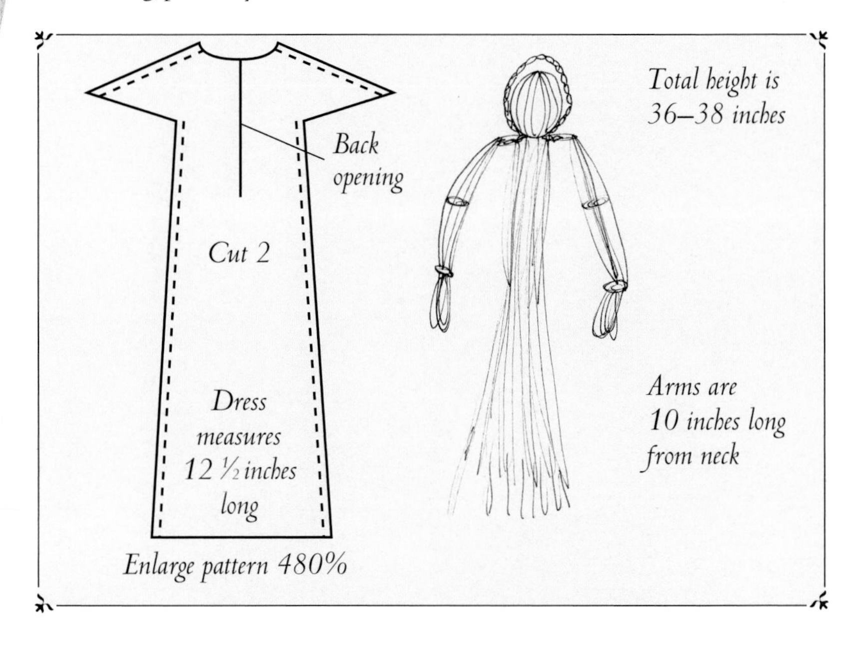

Wedding Ring Pillow

The flower girl won't be the only little angel to grace the aisle when your ring bearer carries this delicate angel pillow. It makes a thoughtful, inexpensive shower gift that won't be duplicated. Coordinate your ribbon with the wedding colors or simply use white. Be sure to select a nice heart or wing-shaped lace appliqué from a fabric retailer to form the body, head, and wings of the angel.

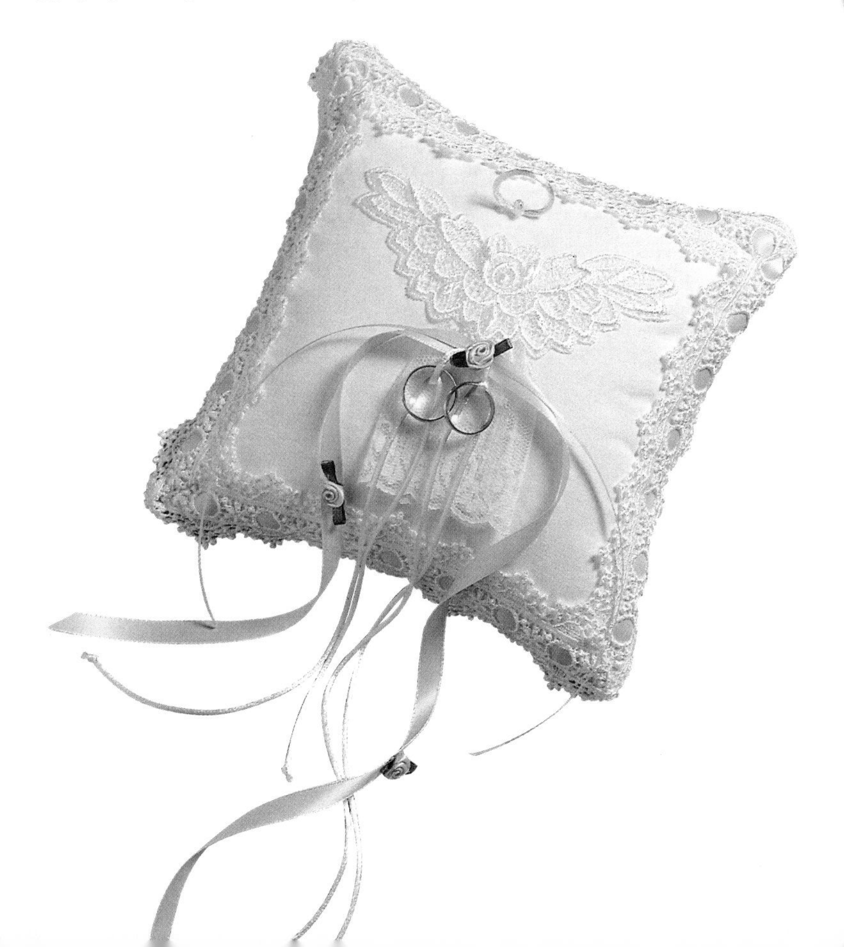

Materials

½ yard good-quality opaque white cotton or linen

9-inch square fusible quilt batting

5-inch lace angel appliqué (purchased)

6 inches of 3-inch-wide lace for skirt

1 small bag polyester batting to fill pillow

1½ yards ¼-inch ribbon

1½ yards heavy white lace with ribbon guides

½ yard each of three different ribbons, cording, or other trims, in coordinating shades

6 to 8 silk rosettes, pearls, or other trimmings of your choice

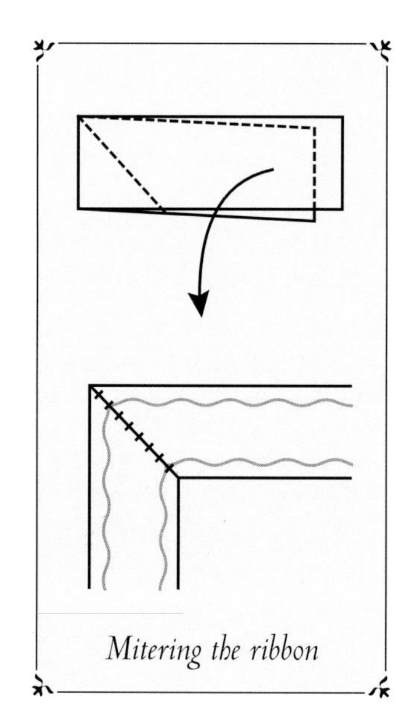
Mitering the ribbon

INSTRUCTIONS

1. Cut three squares of the white cotton, 9 by 9 inches (includes a ½-inch seam allowance). Attach one square to the fusible batting (follow ironing instructions on package) to form the pillow front. The remaining two cotton squares will serve as the doubled pillow back.
2. Blindstitch the lace angel appliqué into position on the pillow front. Use the 3-inch lace to form the angel's skirt, running a small seam down the center back. Stitch the angel appliqué over the skirt waistband, and stitch the skirt to the pillow.
3. Machine-stitch the pillow front to the two backing squares, right sides together, leaving a 5-inch opening for turning and stuffing. Trim the batting to ¼ inch. Turn the pillow right side out and iron gently, using a towel to protect the lace.
4. Fill the pillow with the polyester batting to a gentle firmness, and blindstitch the opening.
5. Weave the ¼-inch ribbon through the heavy lace. Pin in position to all four sides of the pillow, mitering the corners. Hand-stitch the lace to the pillow about 2½ inches from the pillow edge, allowing about ½ inch to hang over. Secure the corners.
6. Use four lengths of the coordinating ribbons or other trims to form ties for the rings (two for each ring), and two more lengths to decorate with rosettes, pearls, or other trimmings.
7. Use a small circle of ribbon to form a halo, if you like. Hand-stitch the halo to the pillow, just above the angel's head.

ANGELIC YARD FLAG

Herald the winter holiday season with this bright house and yard banner. Parachute nylon is widely available from fabric retailers, or substitute any lightweight acetate or nylon lining fabric. Don't expose the flag to harsh weather.

MATERIALS

1 yard parachute nylon or acetate fabric, royal blue, for background, and ¼ yard purple, pink, or white

removable white fabric marker

tracing paper

flesh-color, yellow, or brown fabric scraps for hair; silver or gold for wings

¼-inch heat-bonding tape

sewing thread to match fabrics

small, sharp scissors

gold foil, adhesive, and sealer (Press and Peel)

purchased flagpole

INSTRUCTIONS

1. Cut a piece of the blue background nylon 31 by 41 inches and finish three edges with a ¼-inch turned seam. Turn a 2½-inch pocket at the top of the banner and finish it with another ¼-inch turned seam, as if you were making a café curtain. This pocket will allow you to hang your banner from its pole. The finished banner will be 28 by 40 inches.

Be not forgetful to entertain strangers: for thereby some have entertained angels unawares.

—*New Testament, Hebrews*

2. Enlarge the pattern as indicated (you may have to do this in sections) and transfer onto the banner with the removable white fabric marker. This is your guide for placing and sewing pieces to the flag backing.
3. Trace the individual pattern pieces onto appropriate fabric colors and heat-bond into position on the banner with the ¼-inch heat-fusible tape at each edge. Start with the clouds and then apply the dress, wings, face, and hair, in that order.
4. Using a satin appliqué stitch, machine-stitch around each piece with thread the same color as the fabric or, if you prefer, use black or another single color to do all the stitching. The heat-fusible bond will stop the fabrics from sliding around too much.
5. When all the appliqués have been stitched, turn the banner over to the back. With a small, sharp scissors, remove the blue backing from all the pieces, cutting as close to the stitching as possible without cutting the stitches or the fabric underneath.
6. Using the foil adhesive, draw a long curved horn and freehand star as shown (see photograph on page 45) on one side of the banner, leaving it to cure for 24 hours on a flat surface.
7. Apply the foil by pressing into the adhesive as instructed on the package, and then seal by dabbing sealer onto the foil *only*. Do not allow the sealer to flood onto the fabric as it will stain.
8. When the banner is completely dry, turn it over and apply the adhesive, foil, and sealer to the reverse side of the horn and star. When it's sealed, the banner is ready to hang on your flagpole.

Design measures 24 inches
Enlarge pattern 450%

MATERIALS

4 10-inch pipe cleaners

10-inch Styrofoam cone

hot-glue gun and glue

purchased china doll head and hands

gold spray paint

8-inch round wooden base

2 8-inch lengths thin wire

resin angel wings

¼ yard 4-inch pleated lace

12 inches of 1-inch embroidered ribbon

¼ yard velvet or velour

1½ yards heavy ribbon

½ yard each of two different fine cording or ribbons and metal charms for belt

12 inches sheer 1-inch ribbon for stole

ANGEL DOLL

Make a beautiful angel like this for the pure creative pleasure of designing and dressing her in elegant robes and lace. She will make a lovely addition to your holiday decorations, but you'll probably want to enjoy her all year long.

INSTRUCTIONS

1. Twist four pipe cleaners together to form the arms. Secure at the midpoint to the top of the cone with hot glue, then attach the doll head on top of the arms with more hot glue. Glue the china hands to the pipe cleaner ends.
2. Spray paint the wooden base with gold paint; allow to dry. Affix the cone to the wooden base with hot glue.
3. To secure the wings to the angel, thread a piece of wire through small holes in the wings, then twist around the cone in a figure

eight to hold them securely in place. Reinforce with hot glue.

4. Cover the cone with a layer of lace and glue in place, making sure the bottom edge covers the cone and touches the base. Top with a second layer of lace that is 2 inches shorter. Make two sleeves by running a small seam up additional 2-inch wide pieces of the same lace. Secure the sleeves over the arms, attaching at the shoulder with hot glue. The sleeves will hang to the fingertips.
5. Cut two 4-inch pieces of the embroidered ribbon and crisscross them over the bodice of the doll to form dress top. Glue in position. Use the remainder of the ribbon to make a cummerbund and glue in place.
6. Enlarge the robe pattern as indicated and cut two fronts and one back from the crushed velvet. Make a 3-inch slit in the center back to accommodate the wings. Sew the robe arm and side seams. Use the heavy ribbon to bind the edges around the hem, front openings, and neck of the robe. Turn a ½-inch hem under on the sleeves and trim.
7. After dressing the angel in the robe, secure the back slit over the wings neatly with more hot glue, folding under a smooth edge. Use the cording or ribbon to make a double-tied belt around the waist, and secure charms to belt ties with a drop of glue.
8. Make a halo with a circle of cording, securing it to the back of the head with a drop of hot glue.
9. Drape the sheer ribbon over the angel arms to form a stole. Trim ends into a V.

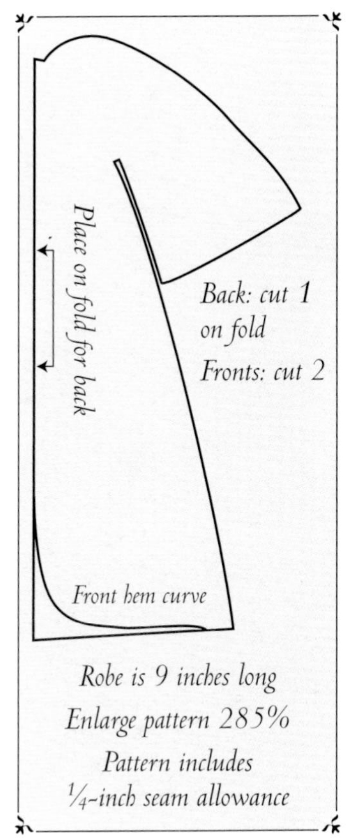

Angel Tree Topper

These tin angels are fun for old-fashioned Christmas trees decorated with cranberry and popcorn strings. They're easy to make and look good in the natural tin color or weathered to a darker patina.

Materials

masking tape

8 by 10-inch sheet of hobby store tin

pencil

wooden work surface (an old cutting board will do)

tacking nails (optional)

rubber mallet

tin punch or awl

tin snips

coarse steel wool (optional)

soldering iron and solder

patina finish and brush (optional)

Instructions

1. Use the masking tape to cover the edges of the tin sheet. This will protect your hands. Enlarge the pattern on page 52 as indicated. Cut out and trace onto the tin with a pencil.
2. Secure the tin to a wooden work surface with masking tape or tacking nails.
3. With the rubber mallet and tin punch, punch out the design, starting in the middle of the design and carefully positioning the punch. Use a single firm stroke to strike with the mallet. Practice on a scrap piece of tin first, to get used to the feel of the mallet and the amount of pressure you need to exert.
4. Follow the dot pattern until you have completed the entire design. Remove from the work surface and cut out the angel with tin snips. Be careful of the edges, which can be sharp. Smooth the rough edges with coarse steel wool, if you like.
5. Cut a rectangular piece of tin about 2 by 5 inches and form into a tube shape, allowing about 1 inch of overlap. Solder the overlapped edges together and allow to cool.
6. Carefully attach the tube to the back of the angel with more solder. Try not to let the solder come through the punched holes onto the angel's front.

7. When the solder has cooled, you may wish to brush on a patina finish to achieve a darker, antique look. Otherwise, simply wash the angel in soapy water, dry thoroughly, and place on the top of your Christmas tree.

Every man contemplates an angel in his future self.

—Ralph Waldo Emerson

RIBBON BOOKMARK

This sweet angel will mark your place in a favorite book while you're busy making more angels for stocking stuffers and hostess gifts. It's a great way to use wood scraps.

INSTRUCTIONS

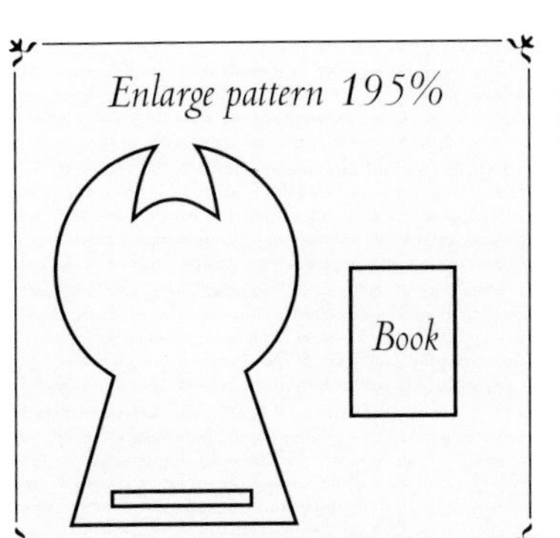

1. Trace the patterns onto the piece of wood. With a jigsaw, cut out one angel and two books. Sand all sides well with fine sandpaper. Wipe off all traces of dust and grit.
2. Paint the angel in colors you like, and books in coordinating colors.
3. Run the grosgrain ribbon through the slot in the angel skirt and overlap 2 inches. Stitch the ribbon together by hand or machine.
4. Glue a book to each side of the ribbon, at the bottom.

MATERIALS

2 by 3-inch piece of ash or other wood, ¼ inch thick

jigsaw

fine sandpaper

brushes and acrylic paints in various colors, including metallic gold

14-inch piece ⅝-inch grosgrain ribbon

needle and thread

white craft glue

HALO OF FLOWERS AND GOLD

MATERIALS

wire clothes hanger

wire cutter or pliers

3 bunches dried and/or silk flowers in colors you like together (purple statice, strawflowers, globe amaranths, and rosebuds all work well)

3 small bunches silk flower greenery, ivy, or similar vines (1-inch leaves or smaller)

green florist tape, ½ inch wide

12 2-inch pieces gold ribbon or braid

½ yard each of red, purple, and gold ribbon, ⅝ to 1 inch wide

Make a halo for the special little angel in your life. She'll find it fun to wear in the Christmas pageant, as part of a Halloween costume, or any dress-up time. It also makes a lovely headpiece for bridesmaids at an outdoor, informal, or country wedding and fresh flowers can be substituted for the dry.

Instructions

1. Measure around the child's forehead, then cut the wire hanger to the same length plus 2 inches to allow for joining at the back. Make the joint using wire cutters or pliers to bend each end into a U shape. Hook the U's together and twist several times to secure. The raw ends will be covered at the end of the project.
2. Cut small sprigs of flowers and greenery and lay them out in piles of like pieces, in any order you desire. Each pile should have about the same amount of greenery and flowers.
3. Start assembling the halo by twisting the end of the florist tape around the wire circle. Hold the wire in one hand, using the other to twist the tape. After you have about 1 inch of taped wire, add a sprig of greenery, stem end first. Give a half-twist of tape and then add a flower sprig. Continue in this manner, covering the stems of each sprig with the foliage of the next and securing each added sprig with florist tape. Every inch or so, add one of the 2-inch pieces of gold ribbon, folded in half, securing the cut ends into the tape. Or use braid instead of the ribbon.
4. Repeat the same pattern all the way around the wire circle, leaving 2 inches at the back covered with tape alone. Cover the wire joint completely.
5. Cut three or more lengths of the red, purple, and gold ribbon to 12 or 14 inches. Fold 1 inch over and secure with a needle and thread to the back, over the covered wire joint. Your angel's halo is ready to wear.

Where love abounds,
angels hover overhead.

—*Anonymous*

Materials

1½ yards quilted material or felt, 60 inches wide

sewing scissors

4 yards lace or pleated bias-tape edging

heat-bonding tape

3 Velcro fasteners

1 yard heat-bonding material

¼ yard each of 4 or more cotton fabrics: flesh color, brown or yellow for hair, at least two miniprints or plaids for dresses, and white or cream lace for wings

permanent fabric markers or embroidery floss

fine point craft fabric paints to match fabrics

gold foil, adhesive, and sealer (Press and Peel)

Christmas Tree Skirt

A joyous group of angels circle the tree awaiting the placement of gifts on Christmas Eve. This is an easy project for the nonsewing crafter, fun and easy to complete in just two evenings.

Instructions

1. From the quilted material, cut a circle at least 46 inches in diameter. If you use a large tree with a larger water pan, you will want to adjust the circle for the skirt up to as much as 58 inches. Slash a straight line to the center of the circle and cut a smaller 7-inch circle in the center to fit around the tree trunk.
2. Bind the inner and outer edges of the skirt and the opening with the lace or bias-tape edging. Use heat-bonding tape, or sew it on if you prefer. Stitch the Velcro fasteners in position at the top, bottom, and center of the opening.
3. Enlarge the angel and holly patterns on page 58 as indicated. Trace 5 angels and 10 to 12 holly sprigs onto the paper backing of the heat-bonding material, flopping the holly pattern for half. Apply the bonding to the selected fabrics and cut out. (Follow the instructions for heat-bonding on the package if you are unfamiliar with this product.)
4. Remove the paper backing and place the angel pieces in position around the skirt as shown, centering the first one on the skirt front. The opening should be at the center back. Heat-fuse the angel pieces in position, beginning with the face and then adding the dress, wings, and hair, in that order. Use permanent

fabric markers to add eyes and mouth to each angel face, or stitch on with embroidery floss. Fuse the holly sprigs among the angels.

5. Using the fabric paints, run a thin bead of paint around the raw edge of each bonded fabric piece, selecting the closest color. Allow to dry on a flat surface for 24 hours.
6. Use the foil adhesive to paint hearts, horns, or other instruments onto the angels in the positions shown in the photograph. Make holly berries from this adhesive also. Allow it to cure for 24 hours, again on a flat surface. When it is clear and sticky, gently press the foil directly onto the adhesive with your finger and pull back the clear plastic film, leaving the gold foil in place. You can go over any spots you missed a second or third time.
7. Carefully dab a clear coating of sealer onto all the gold-foil decorations with the applicator and allow to dry well.

Angel and Pine Tree Quilted Wall Hanging

A combination of appliqué and pieced block handquilting, this Christmas wall hanging is perfect for over the fireplace. You could select colors to match your room decor and leave it up all year long. This project adapts well to lap quilting.

Materials

- acrylic or cardboard for pattern pieces
- 1 yard printed cotton fabric for trees
- 1/4 yard printed cotton fabric for tree trunks
- 1/4 yard printed cotton fabric for angel
- blue erasable marker
- 1 yard quilt batting
- 2 yards plain muslin fabric, preshrunk
- quilting needles
- heavy-duty quilting thread
- scraps of cotton fabric for halo and appliqué hearts
- 4 yards purchased quilt-binding for edges
- antique buttons, lace, or charms
- 3 plastic curtain rings for hangers

For Angel Block Cut:

2 of #1 Dark Green
1 of #1 Gold
1 of #1 Light Cream
2 of #2 Light Cream
2 of #2 Dark Green
2 of #3 Dark Green
1 of #4 Flesh
2 of #5 Red
1 of #6 Red

For Pine Tree Cut:

1 of #7 Red
1 of #8 Dark Green
1 of #9 Green
2 of #10 Light Cream
2 of #11 Light Cream
14 of #12 Dark Green
15 of #12 Light Cream

Instructions

1. Enlarge the two quilt block patterns as indicated. Trace the patterns onto acrylic or cardboard, adding a ¼-inch seam allowance to all sides of each piece. (You also need to allow ¼ inch as turnunder for the appliqué pieces.)
2. Place your pattern pieces on the straight grain of the fabric and draw around the pieces with the blue erasable marker.
3. Cut out the number of pieces needed for each block.
4. Hand- or machine-stitch nine 9½-inch blocks. You need one angel and eight pine trees. Assemble the quilt top, machine-stitch with ½-inch seams, and press all seams well.
5. Cut out a 27½-inch square of quilt batting and plain muslin for the backing. Sandwich the batting between the pieced front and the backing. Press and pin securely, or run several long basting threads through the quilt top to keep it from shifting.
6. Place the hanging in a large or small table quilting frame to keep it taut as you quilt each piece according to the quilting pattern, opposite. Quilt with small running stitches through all the layers of the hanging, starting with the center block and moving outward toward the edges.
7. Press ¼-inch turnunder hems around each of the heart and head appliqué pieces, and pin in position on each block. Using a blindstitch, appliqué all pieces. Add quilting for the eyes, if you like.
8. Hand- or machine-stitch the quilt binding around the four outer edges, mitering the corners for a smooth finish.

9. Give the hanging a tea bath to give it an old-fashioned look, if you like. To make a tea bath, combine 1½ quarts of water and 6 to 8 tea bags in a teapot. Brew the tea for 20 minutes until it comes to a boil, and then cool completely. Soak the hanging in the tea bath for 2 or 3 minutes, checking it carefully to judge color intensity. It will look darker when wet. Rinse and dry flat.
10. Trim the angel with antique buttons, lace, or charms.
11. Hand-stitch curtain rings to the top and side corners, about 1 inch from the outside edge.

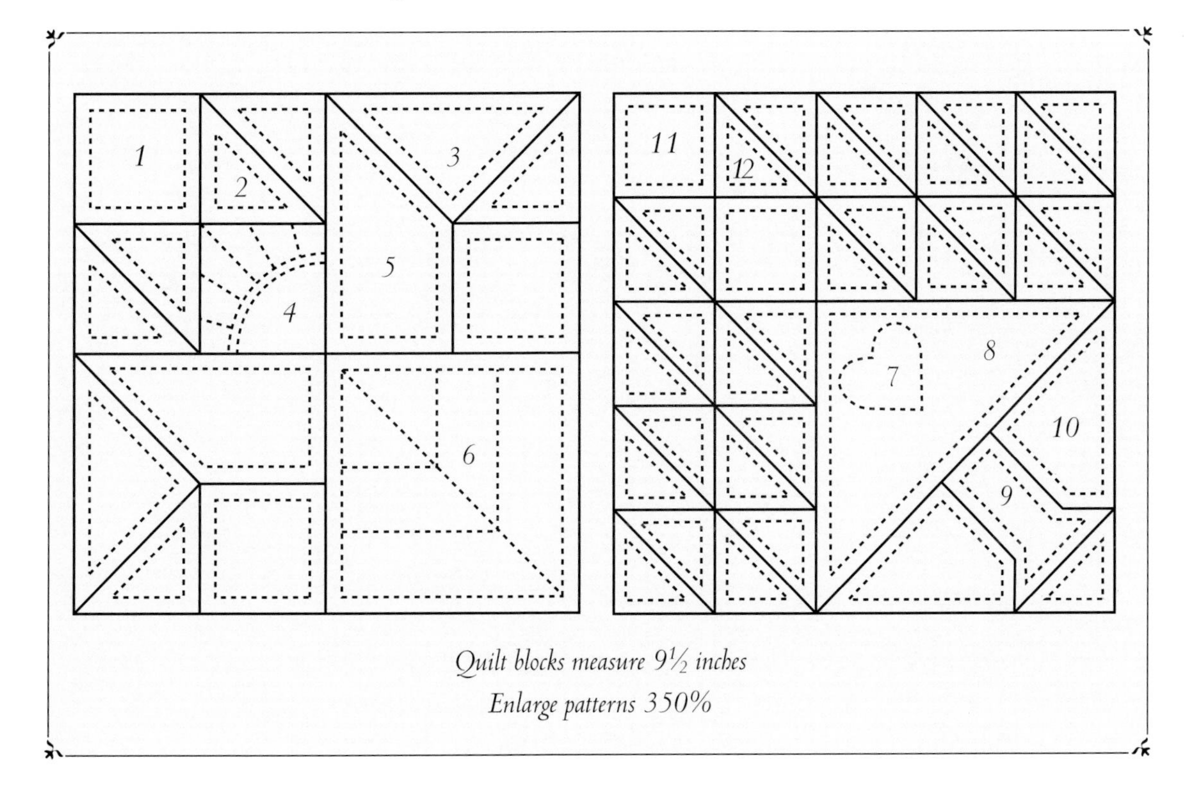

Quilt blocks measure 9½ inches

Enlarge patterns 350%

ANGEL BLESSING BOX

MATERIALS

purchased fiberboard box

gold spray enamel paint

⅓ yard velveteen or other lining fabric

white craft glue or spray fixative

paper angels from greeting cards, wrapping paper, etc.

sewing or nail scissors

clear acrylic spray coating

hot-glue gun and glue

dried or silk flowers, greenery, seed pearls, metal ornaments, or other trimmings

2 yards good quality fabric ribbon or braid in coordinating color

A place to store those little blessings of life—an encouraging note or card, a special keepsake or memento, or some other reminder of past good times, this is also a unique gift for new mothers or newlyweds that needs no wrapping. See page 2 for another version that uses dried rose buds and seed pearls for a different look.

INSTRUCTIONS

1. Spray the box and lid with one or two coats of the gold enamel paint in a well-ventilated area. Allow to dry for several hours.
2. Cut the velveteen or lining fabric to the exact size of your box base, plus an extra ½ inch. Check the fit and then attach the fabric with craft glue or spray fixative to the inside bottom of the box and ½ inch up the sides. While this is drying, cut the side panels, allowing a ½-inch turnunder hem at the exposed rim of the box, and a ¼-inch turnunder at the bottom. Glue the side panel fabric to the walls of the box, paying special attention to a smooth finish at the upper rim. Repeat for the lid, if you like.
3. Carefully cut out the paper angels using fine sewing or nail scissors. Arrange the cutouts on your box lid and sides. Be sure you are satisfied with the placement of the cutouts before applying glue and adhering them to the box surface.
4. Use two or three coats of the spray acrylic coating to protect the box surface. Dry well between coats.
5. Hot-glue any flowers, greenery, or other trimmings onto the box lid and sides in a pleasing pattern. Hot-glue on the ribbon or braid to finish both the top and bottom edges.

Sources for Materials and Supplies

The materials used in these projects are available from any large craft and hobby retailer. Local fabric stores will have parachute nylon or similar fabrics if you ask. Most towns have a stained-glass supplier, often listed under Art Glass in the Yellow Pages of the telephone directory, who will provide glass-cutting supplies and multitudes of beautiful glass to choose from. They are often willing to teach beginners the basics of glass cutting. If you have problems securing supplies locally, write or call these suppliers.

PAINT, SEALERS, ANTIQUING GLAZES

Accent Products Division
Lake Zurich, IL 60047
(708) 540-1604

QUILTING SUPPLIES

The Quilter's Sourcebook
Vermont Patchworks
Box 229
Shrewsbury, VT 05738
(802) 492-3590

GRAPEVINES, DRIED FLOWERS, CORN HUSKS

Dorothy Biddle Service
U.S. Route 6
Greeley, PA 18425–9799
(717) 226-3239

DRIED FLOWERS, ROSEBUDS, BULK SPICES

The San Francisco
Herb Company
250 14th Street
San Francisco, CA 94103
(415) 861-3018

WIDE SELECTION OF CRAFT SUPPLIES (including Press and Peel foil products)

Lee Wards Creative Crafts
1200 St. Charles Street
Elgin, IL 60120
(708) 888-5800